THE 4 CORNERSTONES FOR STRATEGIC LIVING

Brian A. Holmes

The 4 Cornerstones for Strategic Living
By Brian A. Holmes
© 2016 by Brian A. Holmes. All rights reserved.

Sozo Publishing Group
sozopublishing.com

ISBN 978-0-9966161-2-6
Printed in the United States of America

PREFACE

Many years ago, one of my mentors shared a principle with me. He said, "Life is lived on levels and experienced in stages." As we go through our primary education apparatuses, we move from stage to stage and level to level. This process involves learning, study, application, testing, and ultimately passage to the next level.

One thing we are not taught in school is the concept and value of strategic living. Purposeful living. Intentional living. Most of us were told, "Go to school, get a degree, find a good job with a good company, and you will be successful." This seems to be a commonly accepted (and even promoted) path to fulfillment and success. I just don't buy it! All you have to do is look around and see there are very few people who are truly in their lane, doing what they were created to do. There are so few who have found the joy of realizing the full capacity and potential residing within them. So few have discovered how to live their life by design, fulfill their purpose, and impact their generation.

I wrote this book with *your* "next level" in mind. My desire is for you to escape the crowded space where average and ordinary are the norm. My hope is you will join thousands of others who have said YES to the possibilities and engaged the process of pursuing and becoming all they were created to be. Successful passage requires a willingness to learn, to change, to grow, to address limiting beliefs, and so much more. It will take some work on your part, but the rewards are invaluable.

The *4 Cornerstones for Strategic Living* book is a primer, a simple guide to help you begin this exciting journey. In it I explain the timeless principles so many have followed. I also provide some key building blocks and processes that will catapult you into a greater expression of the person you are designed to be.

I am truly honored to be your coach and mentor. Let's begin!

INTRODUCTION
WONDER OF THE WORLD

The Pyramids of Giza are the only remaining structures of what were once known as the Seven Wonders of the Ancient World. The Seven Wonders, declared as such by Philo, a Greek engineer and writer who lived circa 250 B.C.[1], were man-made monuments people of the ancient world assumed were indestructible and eternal. They included the Hanging Gardens of Babylon believed to have been built by King Nebuchadnezzar II around 600 B.C., the 110- foot bronze statue known as the Colossus of Rhodes, and the 500-foot Lighthouse of Alexandria[2]. Of these amazing architectural and engineering feats, only the Pyramids of Giza endure.

Pyramid builders of old—at least the ones who built the pyramids we see standing still today—started with a four-fold strategy:

- A set of intricately detailed papyrus sketches and drawings (created sans a CAD program) often followed by a scale model of the finished structure;

---

1 *Philo of Byzantium,* https://en.wikipedia.org/wiki/Philo_of_Byzantium (January 2016).

2 *The 7 Ancient Wonders,* http://world.new7wonders.com/?n7w-page=ancient-wonders (January 2016).

- a painstaking, methodical astrological computation process by which they would orient their pyramid with one wall facing true north;
- creating a ground plan that required four *precise* right angles 2,000 years before the development of modern geometry's Pythagorean theorem;
- constructing an almost perfectly level platform laid in a perfect square derived from the four right angles of their ground plan, using hand-cut limestone cornerstones, wood posts and rope or string[3].

Impressed yet?

Of the Giza pyramids, the largest and most famous is the Great Pyramid. One of the first things you notice about the Pyramid's construction is that it's extremely bottom heavy. The four ascending walls of the 481-foot-tall pyramid rest firmly and securely on a foundation that covers more than 13 acres. Each of the four sides of the pyramid is aligned within a .06 percent variation with the cardinal points of our modern-day compass[4]. That means one wall faces almost exactly true north.

---

3 http://www.touregypt.net/featurestories/pyramidorienta-tion.htm (January 2016).

4 Dash, Mike, *Inside the Great Pyramid,* http://www.smithso-nianmag.com/blogs/inside-the-great-pyramid-75164298/?-no-ist (January 2016); *Sacred Sites,* https://sacredsites.com/africa/egypt/the_great_pyramid of_giza.html (January 2016).

What you can't see from the exterior is that this monolith, still standing resolute in the ever-shifting sands of the Sahara Desert, is set on four enormous cornerstones, nestled firmly in the bedrock beneath. Far below the sandy surface, not visible from the outside, are many hundreds of feet of underground passages and mysterious chambers—and the all-important cornerstones that have supported this wonder for thousands of years.

The four cornerstones upon which more than 6 million tons of rock have rested for thousands of years are so strategically and firmly set that the 13-acre base of the Pyramid is still level to within a half inch at each corner [5]. Apparently, the ancient Egyptian craftsmen understood the paramount importance of cornerstones in building something that would outlive them, their children and their descendants for countless generations.

You were designed for a purpose and are destined for greatness. The influence of the life you strategically build will outlive you, your children and your descendants for countless generations. It's a testament far more precious and awe-inspiring than this mighty, enduring stone structure. Your ability to stand the tests of time in the ever-shifting sands of life will be accomplished

---

5 Ibid.

by digging deep and strategically placing the proper foundational cornerstones.

This "construction manual" is based on what I've defined as "The 4 Cornerstones for Strategic Living." It is your guide to deliberately craft and place the four cornerstones of your life so you will realize the destiny for which you were created. What you can build is a life of fulfillment and success that's beyond your wildest dreams—unless you're someone like me who dreams big! I'm a firm believer each of our lives has been designed by the supreme Architect, the One with the plan; nevertheless, it's up to us to strategically build that life, a life inspiring others now and standing as a wonder for generations to come.

STRATEGIC LIVING: BUILDING A LIFE THAT STANDS FIRM

There's a song we used to sing in Sunday school when I was kid about a wise man and a foolish man, each of whom built houses on rock and sand, respectively, and the ensuing results of their choices. Now, I know the intent of the song was to teach children to build their lives on something more solid than the shifting sands of a world view. I get that, and no doubt, you do too. But here's the piece: Even those who choose a God-centric world view can end up building a life that goes "splat" just like the house built by the foolish man on the sand.

I'll take it a step farther and say *most* people end up with lives that either fall or at the very least don't leave a lasting legacy, not because they don't believe in a Creator who is greater, wiser, and more powerful than them, and not because they are living their lives apart from that belief, but because they fail to live *strategically* and build the kind of life that same Great Architect designed and desires for them. Building a life of significance that stands firm and endures requires more than a set of beliefs. It requires a distinct vision, a carefully crafted plan, a honed set of skills and abilities, and most importantly, the audacity to believe—even if against the odds—that it can be done.

The Egyptian viziers in charge of constructing the Great Pyramid didn't walk casually out to the job site, hammer four posts at what looked to be "pretty close" to four square corners and begin laying millions of pounds of stones on top of each other. There'd be nothing left today of a structure built that haphazardly. There probably wouldn't have been much left of it a few years after it was completed. Sadly, most people have built their life in such an arbitrary, random fashion.

Most go through life doing what everybody else does: Go to school, get a "good job," work for 40 years, retire, take your pension, go home…and wait to die. I don't mean to sound harsh, but the truth is that's how a huge percentage of us go through—and then end—life. Before we know it, time's up and we haven't begun to fulfill even a fraction of the life we had planned. Even knowing we are destined for more, most of us never build the kind of life we are capable of because we lack a strategy.

As we explore The 4 Cornerstones for Strategic Living, let's first define what it means to live strategically. Put simply, it means to live on purpose, to live intentionally, to live having thought through your next steps and where you want to be 5 years, 10 years, 20 years from now. It means having taken the time and expressed the energy to pursue an understanding of who you are and why you're here. It means asking important questions and not giving up until you have the answers:

- Who am I?
- Why am I here?
- What is my calling in life?
- What is the purpose for which I was created?
- Why did I happen to be born when I was and not 20 years earlier or later?
- What people group am I supposed to be making a contribution to?
- What solution am I supposed to be bringing to the world?

This is the mindset and thought process that leads you to a life lived strategically. Living strategically means engaging purposefully in the intentional process of growing, becoming, and actively pursuing the very thing for which you were created.

Now, with that said, I want to share with you that if a person is going to actually come into a full expression, a full experience, live their life to the utmost, so to speak, there are certain things that *must* happen. Success in every single area of your life depends on whether or not you have approached it strategically, whether or not you've approached it intentionally, whether or not you've approached it on purpose. Your family, your friendships and outside relationships, your business associations and endeavors, your career, your money, whether or not you can generate wealth and keep it, all of these things are tied to *strategic thinking*. All of these things require engaging your mind and your heart in the process of formulating a strategic plan and outlook for them. The amount of success you experience in any of these areas—in fact, in all of these areas—is directly proportionate to whether or not you have taken time and given energy to thinking, visualizing, dreaming, and planning.

There's an incredible passage in ancient scriptures that says to write the vision and make it plain so that the person who writes it and reads it can actually run with the plan, succeed, and do well. The point is it's more than just having vision. It's about actually having a strategic approach to all of these areas of life. Part of that strategy involves you writing it down.

In the discovery process of a court case, when each side is presenting evidence to support their side before actually appearing in court, there's an axiom that "If it's not in writing, it didn't happen." In other words, just because you remember something a certain way and say it happened a certain way, if you don't have some sort of physical evidence, a document of some kind, even if it's just a note you made at the time of the occurrence, as far as proving your case is concerned, it never happened. It's just you talking. It means nothing, and it carries no weight.

Applying that same contention to your strategy for life, I'd say, "If it's not in writing, it's not going to happen."

There's a reason the scripture above said to write it out and make it plain. There's an almost mystical power in the written word. There's just something about writing it down that transforms it from a dream to a more concrete reality. You can talk about your plans and dream about your life, but until you put that plan, that dream on paper—or in a computer document—and make it tangible, chances are it's *never* going to happen.

The word strategy is usually associated with battle plans. Graduates from the United States Military Academy at West Point spend years studying the strategies of hundreds of battles dating from as long ago as the Persian and Greek wars (circa 600 B.C.) right up to the battles you'll hear about on tonight's news. Before officers deploy forces, they develop rigorously precise strategies for the battle. They thoroughly understand their objective and develop plans of action that will achieve them swiftly to minimize casualties and loss. You're not going into a life or death battle, but you still need to spend time and energy devising a strategy for your life that achieves your objective concisely and directly. A well thought-out plan will save you years that could be lost in faltering and hesitation.

A strategy is a plan of action. I hope you caught the key word there. If not, it starts with "a" and ends with "n". All the planning, purpose, and intent in the world get you nowhere until you take action. Living strategically is about doing, about being proactive—even aggressive—when it comes to making things happen in your life. As you read on, you will discover how to develop this strategic approach, how to formulate a mindset, a discipline, and the process to actually build a strategic life, a life that is worth living, and then set that plan into action.

It starts with a foundation built on four cornerstones. Specifically, The 4 Cornerstones for Strategic Living:

1. Personal Healing
2. Personal Discovery
3. Personal Development
4. Personal Deployment

You were designed to complete a unique assignment and have a unique impact on the world. These four cornerstones are the foundational process you go through to become the full expression of the potential you possess.

These cornerstones are set in a particular order. The first cornerstone set in the foundation of the Great Pyramid of Giza determined the exact location and integrity of every other cornerstone, and thereby, the millions of other stones set in that vast structure. In the same way, the veracity of your personal discovery will be skewed if the cornerstone of personal healing is skipped or set haphazardly. From there, the other cornerstones and the life you build on them will be off-center, if only minutely. Eventually, that seemingly insignificant discrepancy in your foundation can cause everything built upon it to come falling down. Don't make the dangerous mistake of neglecting any one of these foundational elements.

My passion and purpose in writing this book is to challenge you to reject the status quo and actively choose to build a life that is strategic and intentional. And if you accept the challenge, I will guide you into the seemingly ever-elusive "how" of making a life of passion and fulfillment a reality. You can be more—so much more—and it all starts right here, right now, with you making the decision to begin to live strategically.

CORNERSTONE #1: PERSONAL HEALING

FINDING AND FIXING YOUR FOUNDATION FRACTURES

Personal Healing is perhaps the most often overlooked and misunderstood building block of strategic living. Most really never think much about the idea of personal healing and the need for it, but it is absolutely essential to creating a successful, prosperous, dynamic life. Every area of your life—vocation, relationships, health (physical, emotional, spiritual), finances—will flourish or fail based on this cornerstone.

Personal healing is the first cornerstone for a reason: You simply cannot become the full expression of all you were created to be until you deal with the inner fractures. The inner fractures are those events you've experienced or even words you've heard that have gone deep into and wounded your soul.

In the foundation of a building, even a small crack left untended can become a chasm that can cause cosmetic and structural damage, sometimes to the point of complete collapse. Where I'm from in Texas the soil is known as black gumbo, a sticky mud you have to experience to understand. It's so sticky when it's wet that dinosaurs were getting bogged down in it 150 million years ago, but so hard when it's dry its compressive strength challenges that of concrete[6]. Believe it or not, that term "black gumbo" is actually a quasi-scientific term used to describe soils that consist of more mud than silt and sand. And the South doesn't have a monopoly on the sticky stuff; it's found as far north as Montana and North Dakota [7].

Building on black gumbo soil requires drilling through many feet of top soil down into the harder rock or shale beneath. Even then, the foundation of structures built in regions of black gumbo will experience shifting as the soil expands and contracts with changes in moisture content. That shifting causes cracks in the concrete slab holding up the weight of the entire building.

People who build in such areas know to be on the lookout for small cracks on their interior walls or in their masonry facades. Those observant enough to recognize the small cracks as tell-tale signs of a foundation fracture and have them repaired quickly suffer no ill effects. Those who ignore the signs of trouble and allow the fracture to expand suffer the consequences.

---

6   Healy, Donna, *There's Science Behind Sticky Gumbo Soil*, http://billingsgazette.com/lifestyles/there-s-science-be-hind-sticky-gumbo-soil/article_8c6c31ef-2b94-5122-b52c-7113644c656c.html (January 2016).

7   Ibid.

Those consequences range from something as relatively harmless as the financial expenditure of having to replace the brick façade that's fallen off the exterior of their house to something as catastrophic as having an entire side of a building collapse, destroying the whole structure and perhaps injuring those inside.

Personal healing is about recognizing the signs of a fracture in your soul and taking the immediate, prescribed steps to mend the fissure before it leads to catastrophic failure. Your soul is your inner self, your heart. Your soul contains not only your intellect and emotions, but also your intuitions, your beliefs, your character, your moral compass, and to some extent your personality. The idea of man's soul is not something unique to a Judeo-Christian world view. Philosophers and thinkers as long ago as Aristotle (384–322 B.C.) understood that human beings are more than lumps of breathing, walking, thinking flesh [8]. In fact, all the major religions of the world believe in the human soul and make reference to it in their teachings. You will find references to the soul in the Tanakh, the Koran, the Dhammapada[9], the Bible, and some Hindu texts.

---

8 Lorenz, Hendrik, "Ancient Theories of Soul", *The Stanford Encyclopedia of Philosophy* (Summer 2009 Edition), Edward N. Zalta (ed.), URL = <http://plato.stanford.edu/archives/sum2009/entries/ancient-soul/ (January 2016).
9 A collection of the sayings of the Buddha.

One ancient text says you will be successful in life proportionate to the condition of your soul. Said another way, the condition of your inner self, what's happening on the inside of you, even the unconscious places, determines the outcomes of your life. Whether you're going to be prosperous, succeed and do very well in life or whether you're going to always struggle and strive, constantly be faced with conflict and continually run into obstacles, all of these things are directly linked to the condition of you inner self, the condition of your soul.

Let's think about that. Why would the condition of your soul affect your success in life? If you understand the entirety of your soul—thoughts, emotions, character, beliefs, morals—it makes perfect sense that if those are healthy the end result will be a life that's healthy and prosperous. But if any of those areas are distorted, cracked, or outright broken, it will undoubtedly influence the way you function on a day-to-day basis. For example, if you've suffered a betrayal of some sort that's never properly healed, your daily interaction with others, whether it's in business or relationships or any other area, will come from a basis of distrust. Anything that grows from a root of distrust is going to be unstable and unhealthy.

Your emotional, mental, and spiritual condition becomes the ceiling for how far you can rise in life.

It also becomes the floor from which you fall. If you don't deal with internal issues, at some point you are going to hit a ceiling or threshold you cannot penetrate or go beyond. It's the unresolved and unreconciled issues of life that haunt and hurt you. It's those issues left unaddressed that sabotage your ability to grow, to build, to achieve, or to succeed. This is true in every area of your life—relationships, marriage, family, career, business endeavors, finances, leadership influence—all of these are impacted by whether or not your soul, your internal self is in a proper and healthy place.

Wherever you are in life right now, whatever you do, you need to consider there may be something holding you back. There may be things you determined many years ago you were going to ignore, to shut behind a locked door and never look at again. I understand that, probably better than most. Everyone—no matter who you are—has suffered some sort of pain they'd rather forget. But I'd suggest to you right now those very issues you've chosen to bury and close your eyes to are the ones that *must* be addressed because at some point they *will* become a ceiling for you. If you're dissatisfied with your current condition, if you know in your heart of hearts that where you are in your life today is not everything there is for you, I want to challenge you to consider that your soul deserves to be healed and you deserve to be whole.

There are so many areas of brokenness a soul can experience. The list below is offered as a starting point for you to begin to explore where there may be fissures in your heart that need healing. It's not exhaustive, but I hope it will encourage you to explore the possibility there may be things in your inner self holding you back so you can begin the personal healing process.

- Abandonment
- Divorced parents
- Rejection
- Sexual abuse
- Emotional abuse
- Spiritual abuse
- Lack of affirmation
- Lack of nurturing
- Absence of a parent (Through divorce, death, abandonment, or simply choosing not to be a part of your life)
- Damaging words spoken by an authority figure or loved one
- Betrayal
- Too much too soon (Think of the many entertainment and sports figures who have achieved too much too soon just to have their lives implode.)
- Catastrophic failure (A personal moral failure, business failure, relationship failure that has affected your self-worth.)
- Poor models of intimacy in relationship

These types of negative experiences (and the myriad not listed here) create limiting beliefs. What you believe about yourself and the world around you governs your trajectory and the ultimate outcome of your life. This includes what you believe about love, about friendship, about marriage, about money, about your abilities, about your very identity. The unhealed areas of your heart are internal calibrations limiting how high, how far, and how fast you will go in life.

If left unresolved, these events are cracks in your foundation. You can ignore the signs (i.e., unhealthy relationships, impulsive business decisions, poor money management), but the chasm will continue to grow, unseen but ever-widening, until your façade falls away and the life you've been building collapses on itself. Don't be that person. Instead, be the person who chooses right now to get the first cornerstone down deep in the bedrock where it will stand firm and hold together.

7 Steps To Personal Healing

Here are seven steps to personal healing that will help you address unresolved issues that are holding you back. This list is not meant to be comprehensive, but it will serve as a starting point for laying the first cornerstone in your strategic life. The following seven steps require a response. There is power in writing down your responses. Don't neglect this. You're worth the time and energy it takes.

1. **Acknowledge**: Dr. Phil McGraw is credited with saying "You cannot change what you don't acknowledge."[10] You may have heard this before but never stopped to think it applies to you. In my counseling and coaching I meet people every week who have hidden things away so deeply and for so long, in hopes if they ignore it long enough it will go away, that in many cases they've created a pseudo-reality in which the event never happened. Guess what? It doesn't go away until you deal with it, and dealing with it begins with acknowledging it.

   - Is there anything in the past that happened to you or that you did that you need to acknowledge? There may be several things. Take time and be as thorough as you can.
   - It goes deeper than acknowledging an act or a word. You need to acknowledge, to the best of your ability, how you felt or what you believed because of the experience. It might be shame. It might be anger. It might be regret. Do your best to identify and acknowledge your ensuing emotions and responses.
   - Did it create a limiting belief? If so, what is that belief? Express it as thoroughly as you can.

---

10 *Dr. Phil*, http://www.drphil.com/articles/article/323 (January 2016).

- In what way(s) has that belief limited you? Dig deep into the very core of your beliefs and write down things you've done or not done, said or not said because of a false, limiting belief about yourself or about the world around you.

2. **Confess**: Don't worry, I don't mean for you to get up in front of a group of people and confess all your failures, wrongdoings, and shortcomings. I think we'd all agree there's been enough of that. That's not what I'm talking about at all. Confession is actively bringing these events, words, feelings, and beliefs that have been hidden for so long out into the open. I like to call it bringing them out of darkness and into the light. The mere act of revealing these hidden events, emotions, and beliefs renders them powerless.

   Go somewhere private and secure—or to your closest confidant, *if* you desire—and verbally, out loud recount—even though it might feel awkward—what you acknowledged in Step 1. As you confess these experiences, as you say "This happened to me. This is what I experienced. This person said this to me, and it deeply wounded me. This is how it made me feel. This is what I believed because of it. This is what I did because of what I believed," as you hold them out in the light, something incredible happens: It liberates you from the bondage of that particular situation.

3. **Resolve**: Resolve in your mind you will deal with the pain. You must have determination and tenacity to get through what's ahead. If it makes you cry, weep, groan, lie on the floor and flail around like a two-year-old child who is throwing a temper tantrum, whatever the expression, resolve to allow yourself permission to go through that, then determine you will see it through, no matter how painful it gets. Don't leave this undone. Do this and come out on the other side healed.

4. **Forgive and release**: Most pain any of us experience in life is the result of someone else having imposed that pain on us. That being said, there is nothing, I mean *nothing*, more important than forgiving and releasing the individuals who have caused you harm. To hold a grudge, to be bitter or angry, to actually hate someone and to foster internal conflict and negative emotions all the time against someone is not hurting them; *it is destroying you*. Bitterness is like drinking poison and expecting it to kill someone else. Nine times out of ten, the person who caused you pain has forgotten all about the event you're spending so much time and energy holding onto. You are the one still paying for what *they* did. It defies reason.

You must forgive, and you must release them. This is an act of your will. Only you can carry out this step. You have the ability to release the pain, the anger, the shame, the regret. Don't say "I can't." You can. I know you can because I've been there myself. Whatever it was, let it go and blow the ceiling off of your life. Let *them* go so *you* can be free. The one you're forgiving may never be free. They'll have to live with the consequences of their actions and their decisions, but you can be free from that if you will simply release your heart to say, "I forgive. I'm done with this. I'm not going to hold this any longer. I'm letting it go."

5. **Pray**: No matter your particular faith bent, I encourage you to pray and ask for healing. Ask God for comfort and grace as you process all the thoughts and emotions that accompany the step of inner healing. This process of inner healing will stir in your soul—perhaps for the first time—your need for a power greater than yourself. Pray. You'll be surprised how powerful it is and how well it works.

6. **Receive**: You have to be open to receive healing, forgiveness, and restoration. Look at it this way, when something is broken it takes action to fix it. Someone or something has to put it back together. Once you've confessed, forgiven, released, and prayed, you have to actively open your heart to receive healing, to let the pieces come back together, to let your life be restored to its original value and intent. The miraculous thing is when you pray and

then open your heart to receive healing, restoration can and does happen. You will be amazed as your life begins to transform into its original design. Receive your healing.

7. **Live and become**: Make the conscious, assertive, even aggressive choice to live the life you were created to live, to become all you were created to be. If you're going to go through this process, don't just go through it for the sake of going through it. Do it with the passionate purpose of getting to the point where you can live free and become the full expression of everything for which you were created. You were made for so much more than the status quo. Live and become all you already are!

CORNERSTONE #2:
PERSONAL DISCOVERY
GETTING TO KNOW YOU

Back in the late 1960s there was a popular book by John Powell titled *Why Am I Afraid To Tell You Who I am?*[11]. Powell answers his book's question with the following statement: *"I am afraid to tell you who I am, because, if I tell you who I am, you may not like who I am, and it's all that I have."* That may or may not be a legitimate answer to the author's question, but underlying the thesis of his book is the more fundamental problem that most people aren't able to reveal their true identities to others—possibly even to themselves—because they have absolutely no idea who they are or why they're here. Most go through life never taking the time to discover their true identity and the innate gifts, talents, skills, and abilities that make them who they are.

The pursuit of true identity is a theme as old as time and has been expounded upon in philosophy, religion, and literature. It was the ancient Greek philosopher Aristotle who said "Knowing yourself is the beginning of all

---

11 Powell, John. *Why am I afraid to tell you who I am?: Insights into personal growth.* Allen, TX: Thomas More, 1969.

wisdom"[12]. In the Bible's Old Testament (Genesis 32), the Hebrew patriarch Jacob struggled through a time of darkness in his life before coming to the realization of his true identity as Israel, the father of today's nation of the same name. In his award winning book, *Invisible Man*, Ralph Ellison lasers in on this overwhelmingly important issue: "I was looking for myself and asking everyone except myself questions which I, and only I, could answer. It took me a long time and much painful boomeranging of my expectations to achieve a realization…that I am nobody but myself…When I discover who I am, I'll be free"[13].

Personal Discovery, the second cornerstone in strategically crafting your life, is important because until you know who you are and recognize those attributes which set you apart from every other human on the planet, you won't know and understand the "why" of your existence and be able to move toward achieving all you are capable of. Every person is born with a unique design, assignment, and destiny, if you want to use that word. Every person inherently possesses a particular thing they are to contribute to this life. Not only that, but every person possesses the ability to accomplish

---

12 *Goodreads.com,* http://www.goodreads.com/quotes/3102-knowing-yourself-is-the-beginning-of-all-wisdom (Jan 22, 2016).

13 Ellison, Ralph. *Invisible Man.* New York: Random House, 1952.

their particular assignment. There's no one born into any circumstance that is absent of capacity to be great, to do great things, to make significant contributions. You have that power.

The challenge is life teaches us what's possible and what's not possible. As children, we're told "No" maybe hundreds of times each day. Obviously some of those are necessary to protect us, but hearing that word over and over actually trains our minds to think in terms "No" rather than "Yes"; to think in terms of what's not possible rather than what is possible. Without realizing it, we're being conditioned from childhood to believe "Oh, I better not try that because it won't be allowed. Oh, that'll never work out. Oh, somebody won't like it if I do that." We are taught from the time we're born until the time we die to dismiss engaging in any activity that might pose risk or be unacceptable, and in doing so, we learn to dismiss possibility. You have been conditioned your whole life to expect less than what is really possible. Personal discovery requires courageously pushing beyond the restrictive belief system you've developed over time. It takes boldness to look the world square in the eye and shout "Yes!" when it keeps saying "No."

Your life reveals what you believe about who you are, and what you believe about who you are is shaped— or misshaped—largely by things that are said to and about you and by things that happen to you as you grow and mature. Many of these beliefs are completely contradictory to the truth. Wait. Let me put that more simply: They are a lie.

Unwittingly, you've adopted many of these lies about who you are and are living your life based on what you've believed to be truth. At some point, if you're going to discover the truth *as it really is*, you have to challenge the truth *as you've known it*. Personal discovery is about evaluating, discovering, and learning what you have in you, what you really *can* do. This discovery process is the step-by-step, systematic approach to excavating and reviving what is true about you at your deepest level.

In order to reclaim your original design and destiny, to really get back to what is possible, you need a real-life reboot. Rebooting a computer is sort of like clearing a traffic jam. If you think of the RAM (random access memory) of your computer as a highway and all the programs running on it as cars, when you get too many cars on the road or when one of them breaks down, it causes a serious slowdown or outright end of progress. Rebooting your computer gets all the cars off the road. You start back up with all the lanes cleared.

You're born hardwired a particular way with a particular personality and particular strengths and abilities. Life then starts to download things that interfere with you operating as you were designed. You need to reboot. A reboot is a reset, a rediscovery. It's going back to the original condition. Personal discovery is, in fact, the process of investigating and inventorying all the things you have available to you inherently, and then resetting your beliefs and your expectations to the facts as they really are, not as has been downloaded to you through life's identity warping words, events, and experiences. This is fundamental because what you believe to be true about your abilities, about your worth, about your value, about your potential is exactly what you will experience.

"At the center of your being you have the answer; you know who you are and you know what you want," Lao Tzu (601–531 BC, founder of the Chinese philosophy of Taoism)[14].

Most people are unwilling—not unable—to thoughtfully dig deep into the center of their "being" to discover the truth about who they are and what they can truly do. That's why most people will never have a strategy that leads to a life of accomplishment, satisfaction, and success.

---

14 "Lao Tzu (Laozi)," *The Famous People website*,//www. thefamouspeople.com/profiles/lao-tzu-226.php (January 2016).

There are five parts to the personal discovery process. Below is a list of these five parts to serve as the groundwork from which you can begin the process. An important part of this process is inventorying your discoveries.

1. **Understand your personality**. You came into this world with a specific set of characteristics and traits that make you unique from every other person alive now, in the past, and in the future. It's what makes you you. It's your personality style, your propensities toward how you view life, how you engage with people, how you interface with opportunities. Your first step in personal discovery is to learn your personality style.

   Discovering your specific personality style allows you to begin to understand the how and the why of your day-to-day interactions, personal and vocational, as well as understand the what and the where of your next steps in strategic living. For example, someone with an extroverted personality style might not find satisfaction working in a vocation where they sit at a desk review data on spreadsheets, but that same task can be very satisfying to someone with a more reserved, thoughtful personality. Understanding your personality helps you craft a strategy that will lead to success in all arenas.

2. **Recognize your strengths and passions**. There are some things in life you are inherently good at, they just

come easy for you, and for as long as you can remember you've had that particular gift, talent, or skill. These are your core competencies, and you need to be aware of what they are because they are at the center of finding your purpose in life. Just as important as those things you are innately gifted in are those things about which you are passionate. Don't make the mistake of discounting the importance of your passions. In the same way you are born with a bent toward a particular personality style and with specific strengths, you also come prewired with certain passions. Passions go hand in hand with your strengths in finding and achieving the life for which you were originally created.

Dr. Jonas Salk, inventor of the polio vaccine, combined his conscientious personality, his natural analytical strength, and his passion for stopping crippling, killing diseases. Because of him, polio is close to being eradicated worldwide. Your strengths and your passions work in concert to achieve your overall purpose and destiny.

3. **Identify your core values**. Your core values are those principles, ideals, and morals that drive your decisions. They are the non-negotiable ideals to which you automatically default when making choices that affect your destiny. Your core values will determine the trajectory of your journey. They will guide you in resolving problems, dealing

with conflict, creating alliances, making business decisions. They will determine how you spend your time, your money, and your energy. Take the time to analyze your choices to identify your core values.

4. **Clarify your vision**. There's an old proverb that says "Without vision, the people perish." Your vision is what connects you to something larger than yourself and compels you to move toward your goals. A piece of fruit once picked from the tree or vine from which it sprouts immediately starts to decay. The decomposition process takes time, but if left sitting on a table for a few days, that piece of fruit, now disconnected from its life source, will start to shrivel and eventually rot, decay, perish. It dies from the inside out because it's no longer connected to anything more substantial than itself.

Without a clear and compelling vision for where you're going next week, next month, this year, the next five years, the next ten years, you're much like that piece of fruit sitting on a table waiting to rot; you're dying from the inside out. To stay connected to your life source you absolutely must have a vision for what you want your life to be, what you are trying to achieve and accomplish in the time you have here.

Your vision needs to be specific, compelling, and declared. You may need some time to yourself to clarify your vision. Once a year, I take a personal "vision retreat" where I physically go away for a time, unplug from everything, and I dream. I think. I plan. I bring my heart and my mind to a place where I can really focus on what I want and where I'm going.

Walking around with a head full of daydreams is not a vision. I told you earlier about an ancient text that says to write the vision and make it clear. You need something concrete you can refer to, to keep you moving toward your goal. You can refine your vision as you grow, but it starts with clarifying what you want your life and legacy to be.

5. **Strategically execute your plan**. Once you understand your personality and how you're wired, you recognize your strengths (talents, skills, gifts, abilities) and your passions, you identify your core values, and you clarify a compelling vision for your life, it's time to take those components and use them as a road map, first, to see where you're going, and second, to tell you how to get there. Take the time to write down all you've learned about yourself in these four areas of discovery. As you examine each area and how each relates to the others, you'll begin to formulate a picture of who you were created to be and what you were created to do. The picture may see a little out of focus at first, a little fuzzy around the edges, but as you get to know yourself on

a deeper level through using these tools, the vision will become more and more clear and you'll be able to run with it.

CORNERSTONE #3: PERSONAL DEVELOPMENT

YOUR HIGHEST RETURN ON INVESTMENT

I love basketball. When I was a young man I loved playing it, and while I don't spend much time as an adult watching any professional sports, professional basketball players impress me more than any other professional athletes. To me, they embody true athleticism. They are fast, strong, and smart. They possess amazing endurance and lightning-fast reflexes. They have precision-honed skills born from years and years and years of practicing the same shot over and over and over.

Michael Jordan is undoubtedly one of the best to ever play the game of basketball. He's not only the most decorated player in the history of the game, having helped the Chicago Bulls win six National Basketball Championships, he's also a former Olympic athlete and now a successful businessman[15]. Two things that have been key to his success: He understands the value of failure. He understands the value of personal development.

---

15 *Michael Jordon Biography,* http://www.biography.com/people/michael-jordan-9358066#early-life (January 2016).

"I've missed more than 9,000 shots in my career. I've lost almost 300 games. Twenty-six times, I've been trusted to take the game winning shot and missed. I've failed over and over and over again in my life. And that is why I succeed... I've always believed that if you put in the work, the results will come," [16] Michael Jordan, champion basketball player, Olympian, businessman.

Great athletes cannot just be naturally good at something to play at the professional level. Sure, natural ability is where it usually starts, but to succeed at the highest levels, make the highest incomes, receive the highest accolades, and win the highest honors, they practice. And then when they're done, they practice some more. There are professional golfers who go out and hit a couple thousand balls a day. They throw the ball into the most difficult lie and practice recovering from that position a couple hundred times.

And it's not just physical work. Elite athletes meet with coaches, trainers, and psychologists. They use their minds; they study the game and others who've played it, learning constantly from what's been done prior so they can be the one to define what will be done next. They pour their time and energy into personal development.

---

16   *Michael Jordan Quotes,* http://www.brainyquote.com/ quotes/authors/m/michael_jordan.html (January 2016).

This doesn't make them selfish. It makes them world changers in their chosen arena.

In our culture, the idea of personal development has waned in the last several decades. For most in our culture today, education ends at graduation from high school, or for some, college, and is quickly replaced by entertainment. Our culture conditions us to place a higher value on recreation and entertainment than on feeding our minds and on personal growth. The optimist in me wants to think I see a shift in that trend, to believe that the up-and-coming generation is rediscovering the importance and value of education and development as a lifelong endeavor. Time will tell. One thing I know with certainty is that in any generation if you're going to be a world changer you must learn the importance of pouring into yourself by way of personal development.

I was fortunate. I grew up listening to and reading some of the giants in the field of personal development such as Zig Ziglar, Brian Tracy, Paul J. Meyer, Les Brown, and Earl Nightingale. The principles these men espoused are timeless and universal. Their teachings settled deep in my heart and mind at a young age and have influenced me all my life. For as long as I can remember, I've been passionate about personal development, about tapping into and building that core gift that makes us each unique and enables us each to succeed. Apparently it's part of the way I'm wired, part of my personality, core values, and strengths. It's no surprise as an adult I pursued this as a vocation, and now spend my days traveling the world speaking, writing books, and teaching on the subject.

Knowing your talents, abilities, skills, and gifts is great, but it's not the end game. To continue to strategically build a life of meaning, purpose, and fulfillment—the life for which you were created—you now have to make a commitment to invest your time, energy, and resources into personal development. I don't mean you have to quit your job and enroll in some sort of formal, full-time educational regimen. That might be fine for some, and if so, then go for it, but if that doesn't fit your life, don't be discouraged. There is a timeless principle that applies here. "As a man sows, so shall he reap." When you "sow" into your life in the area of personal development, you "reap" in every area of life. The return on investment you get from any systematic, consistent personal development program is immeasurable and without limit. You'll be stunned at the significant results you can achieve from a modest investment in yourself.

Earl Nightingale, who I referred to above, once said, "One hour per day of study in your chosen field is all it takes. One hour per day of study will put you at the top of your field within three years. Within five years you'll be a national authority. In seven years, you can be one of the best people in the world at what you do." One hour a day. Building a life of meaning and fulfillment, a successful life that outlives you for generations is yours for an investment of one hour a day.

Below is a list of seven ways you can spend your one hour a day in your pursuit of personal development. It's not an exhaustive list but it consists of a number of ways I've found are very helpful and very necessary to set the strategic living cornerstone of personal development.

1. **Become a reader**. You're reading this book so you obviously possess the rudimentary skills to undertake this first step of personal development. I can't stress enough the importance of reading, and here's why: Leaders are readers[17]. Those in the top tier of every discipline—from Hollywood to Wall Street to the White House—all have in common the trait of being readers. Just as Earl Nightingale said it takes one hour a day to become top in your field, to become an expert in any discipline you simply need to read the 10 top books concerning that subject matter. By doing that one thing, you put yourself in the top one to two percent of experts in that field. I include in this category listening to audio books. Audio books are a great way to gain knowledge. You can listen to

---

17 Harry Truman, 33rd President of the United States, "Not all readers are leaders, but all leaders are readers". http://www.truman.edu/about/history/our-namesake/truman-quotes (January 2016).

audio books on your daily commute to that job you find so unfulfilling and at some point have prepared yourself to enter the vocation or profession for which you were created and in which you will find purpose and meaning. If you want to really rise to the top of your game, you have to be a reader.

2. **Pursue education and knowledge on all levels**. This doesn't have to be enrolling in a community college course or some other formal setting, although that is a great resource if it's available. In today's technology rich world, education comes in many forms and by many means. Make it part of your weekly routine to be on the lookout for educational opportunities in the form of online courses, seminars, workshops, lectures. Find them and enroll in them. Gain knowledge in as many ways as you can. Education doesn't happen accidentally. You have to pursue it diligently and enthusiastically.

3. **Make new acquaintances**. Track and field athletes training for a race don't go to the track and run with those they know they can beat. They choose a lane next to a runner faster than them. It's a proven strategy for success. Make a concerted effort to become acquainted with those who are presently doing what you want to do at a high level, and then spend time with them whenever possible—without becoming a pest or stalking. Surround yourself with

people who are already one or two or ten steps ahead of you. You'll soon find yourself leading the pack.

4. **Hire a personal coach**. There's an old Chinese proverb that says "A single conversation with a wise man is better than ten years of study." Utilizing the services of a personal coach is one of the best ways to jump-start your success in any area. Some of the greatest things I've ever learned, greatest areas of growth I've ever experienced were when I brought someone alongside me and was willing to pay them for their expertise, guidance, counsel, and insights. Believe me, they have spent many years and paid a heavy price to get where they are. The wisdom they've gleaned has cost them dearly, but is priceless for you. Life coaching is a proven way of attaining real results in any endeavor because it draws out the very best of who you are and enables you to make decisions that will improve your life. Make the investment in yourself. Yes, it will cost you some money, but they are worth it, and more importantly, so are you.

5. **Attend conferences related to your dream or your aspiration**. This is not the same as attending lectures and seminars. Larger in scope and attendance, conferences offer countless more opportunities. Not only do they provide a venue for you to be challenged and inspired by what others in your field

are doing, they're also a great place to showcase your unique services and abilities. The greatest advantage to attending conferences is the networking they provide. They allow you to meet experts and mentors and form strategic connections.

6. **Foster key relationships**. To succeed you need two things: Resources and relationships. If you have to choose between the two, always choose relationships because the right relationships will open doors to resources. Racing in the lane next to the fastest runner is not the same as training one-on-one with them. The first will draw you forward fast; the second can completely change the trajectory of your life. The right relationship can take you places you never dreamed you'd go. Foster friendships with those who sharpen your skills, fuel your passion, and enlarge your vision; those that challenge you to keep pushing toward your goals.

7. **Listen**. Just as you learned limiting beliefs about yourself from the countless voices in the world that said "No," you can unleash your potential by purposefully seeking out and listening to those that say "Yes!" And while there are varying ideas about how many times you have to hear something for it to take hold and become part of your psyche, part of your life view, before it can start to change you from the inside, the truth is there is no hard number—

except it's more than one. Learning to believe in what you can do requires repeatedly listening to the right voices. Fill your mind with audible input that will condition you to think in a particular direction by listening to Podcasts, CDs, downloads of those whose wisdom and experience will lead you and encourage you to reject the status quo and push on toward your particular vision. And then do it again and again and again. You get the picture. It took a lifetime for you to learn all the things the world has said you can't do. Devise a strategy and make the time to listen to the voices of truth that say "Yes, you can!"

CORNERSTONE #4:
PERSONAL DEPLOYMENT
WHAT CUMMINGS SAID

It's in deployment that greatness is revealed. There comes a time when planning becomes redundant, and it's time to engage in working the plan so the plan can work. The United States boasts the best, most advanced military in the world. The men and women of our armed forces go through rigorous training to become the best soldiers on the planet. But all their physical, mental, and psychological training are absolutely worthless until they're deployed. Until they are activated and sent into a specific place for a specific job, all their training, preparation, and planning is for naught.

The only winners in life are the ones who get in the game, go all in, and refuse to look back. The final cornerstone of personal deployment is what separates the winners from the whiners, the doers from the dreamers. You see, it's possible to have complete clarity about who you are and why you're here, to have refined the vision for your life until it's crystal clear, to have attained a complete education and all the training necessary for you to succeed but still fail to realize your full potential and achieve your full measure of success. The good news is I can tell you how to be sure that doesn't happen to you.

There are some armchair quarterbacks who know as much about the game as the coaches on the sidelines. They can predict a blitz, when to run the ball, when to pass—all from the safety and comfort of their living room. Some of them are even naturally gifted athletes whose skills and abilities at the top of their game rivaled those of the players whose names and numbers are the stuff of legends. The reason they're the ones working a nine-to-five, living paycheck to paycheck and not the ones with $100-million-plus contracts boils down to one thing: Fear. Not the fear of injury, of being blind-sided, sacked, and ending up with a broken collar bone. The kind of fear I'm talking about is the same fear that paralyzes most people today—maybe you. It's the fear of failure, or just as common, the fear of success.

Most never suit up and walk out onto the field of life because they are frozen by fear. Nine times out of ten that fear is born from an untended fracture in your foundation that prevents you from trusting in yourself. Self-distrust is the natural offspring of a belief system that says you can't when the reality is you can. Self-distrust creates excuses. Self-distrust blinds you to what's possible. Self-distrust imprisons you in indecision and hesitation, the mother and father of failure.

American avant-garde poet E. E. Cummings wrote "It takes courage to grow up and become who you really are." Courage is what personal deployment is about; the courage to face your fear of failure, of success, of losing relationships, of other people's opinions, of losing your financial stability—the blinding, paralyzing, dream-destroying fear of the great unknown.

The United States of America exists today because a handful of men meeting in Faneuil Hall in Boston faced some very real fears, and nevertheless, chose action rather than paralysis. Faneuil Hall was the old town meeting place of Boston in the 1700s. It's where John Adams, Sam Adams, Paul Revere, Robert Newman and other colonial leaders had the first conversations about breaking free from English rule and forming an independent country. It's where the *idea* of America was born. At the time, speaking of such an idea was treason, punishable by death. It took courage to even broach the subject publicly.

Ideas are nothing more than air until someone acts on them. These men had the idea of a country ruled by a government elected by and for the people. They had the courage to discuss this idea. A few years later they and others had the audacity to pen the idea into the *Declaration of Independence*. The authors of this document knew they were declaring war on the greatest power in the world. Afraid? You bet they were. Did they live to regret it? No. As a matter of fact, most of them lived to see their idea become a reality. And their names and their legacy live today, almost three hundred years later, because they faced their fears and chose not to hide in the upper floor of a meeting hall and continue to dream and plan and think about how wonderful such a country could be. They chose to deploy their dream and make it reality.

All great ideas carry with them an element of fear. You have a great idea. Maybe many. Are you afraid of what might happen if you act on them? Sure, you are. That's not the question. The question is whether you're going to purposefully choose to act in spite of those fears.

Will it be difficult? Rolling downhill is easy. It takes no effort at all because gravity does all the work. Climbing up is always hard. Yes, it will be difficult.

Will there be elements of loss? I promise if you pursue success, if you pursue fullness in your life, you will lose some of your current relationships. Not everybody is meant to go with you to the next level. Will it be worth it? Without a doubt!

> *"Knowing is not enough; we must apply. Willing is not enough; we must do"* Johann Wolfgang von Goethe.

I'm a licensed pilot, not by profession but by passion. Aviation is one of my passions. No surprise, it also plays a role in fulfilling my purpose. When I board a plane, I'm not like the typical passenger, looking for my seat, stowing my stuff, settling in to wait for the ride to be over. My mind is racing, wondering how much fuel the aircraft holds, how fast it can go, what altitude we'll be flying. I have to tell you, I get really excited every time I get on an airplane—which is quite a lot.

As a pilot I understand the importance of filing a flight plan, I know the purpose of the instruments, appreciate the tremendous potential of the aircraft, and have mastered all the skills needed to fly it, but until I engage the engine, accelerate and pull back on the stick to actually leave the ground, all that knowledge and understanding is fruitless. It means nothing. I can taxi around on the runway for hours going nowhere. I have the potential to travel anywhere in the world, but until I take the action necessary to deploy the possibilities inherent in that airplane, I'm stuck on the tarmac.

What you *do* is what matters. If the brave men meeting in Faneuil Hall had never done more than talk about their idea and plan further meetings, we'd be singing *God Save the Queen* at a cricket match instead of *God Bless America* at a baseball game. If the brave men and women of our armed forces are never deployed, their training is meaningless and our country is unprotected from its enemies.

The world is waiting for you to show up. Until you leave the comfort of dreaming, planning, and training and get in the game, you'll never know what you're capable of. Someone right now needs the solution you bring to the table. Someone right now is looking for an answer you have. Someone right now is looking for the product you represent.

It is your time for deployment. You know what to do. You've discovered your true self and all your gifts and abilities. You have a plan. You've worked hard. You've prepared. You've invested the time and energy. You've done the training, read the books, gone to the conferences. You have a dream and a vision for your life and for your future. If you're waiting for somebody to tell you now is your time, here I am. Consider yourself told. Write that book. Start that business. Buy that property. Do that deal. Get in the game, go all in, and never look back.

CONCLUSION

Review

Let's go over these one more time. The 4 Cornerstones for Strategic Living are:

1. Personal Healing
2. Personal Discovery
3. Personal Development
4. Personal Deployment

As you likely have deduced, these cornerstones should be laid in a particular order. While you can do the semantics of discovery, development, and deployment, if you have not taken the time to pursue personal healing, you are building on a faulty foundation. You may very well experience levels of success, but the unresolved issues will eventually show up and limit your ability to realize your full potential.

As any good engineer or architect knows, a structure's integrity and value depends on a well-engineered foundation. Each of these cornerstones is critical to your long-term success and fulfillment.

Action Plan

1. Decide you will live a Strategic Life

2. Hire a counselor, coach, and/or connect with a mentor who can help you with each part of the process
3. Invest in yourself
4. Connect with our growing community of Strategic Leaders (see below)
5. Attend a live event with me

Connect Online

We invite you to connect with us online at

BrianHolmes.com

There you will find a virtual treasure trove of resources for any individual desiring to grow their life and leadership.

- The Monday Mastery Video Series
- Blog Posts, Articles, and other Training Resources
- The Strategic Leader Podcast
- And much more!

Be sure to subscribe to our E-Mail updates, and we will keep you informed concerning new content, live events, webinars, and other opportunities offered by our company.

Coaching and Training

For more information on Brian Holmes' coaching and training opportunities, you may visit our website or contact us at support@brianholmes.com.

Your Next Step

I have produced a five-session online video course on the 4 Cornerstones for Strategic Living. In order to dive deeper into this study, and to take your life and leadership to the next level, visit **BrianHolmes.com/4CS**.

40007932R00034

Made in the USA
San Bernardino, CA
09 October 2016